Sydney
Rock Pools

For my wife Lucy, for showing me this beautiful country and supporting and believing in my dreams.

For my family and friends in Spain.

For Rafa and Leo.

SYDNEY
ROCK POOLS

PHOTOGRAPHS BY IGNACIO PALACIOS

First Published in 2014 by Ignacio Palacios Photography

National Library of Australian
Cataloguing-in-Publication data
Author: Ignacio Palacios
Title: Sydney Rock Pools
ISBN: 978-0-646-915852 (hard back)

Photographs by Ignacio Palacios,
www.iptravelphotography.com.au
Design by Kathie Eastway
Image preparation/editing by Ignacio Palacios

Printed in Hong Kong by Toppan Printing

info@iptravelphotography.com.au
www.iptravelphotography.com.au

Newport rock pool at sunset

Introduction

BY IGNACIO PALACIOS

I have been photographing ocean pools since I came to Sydney in 2008. In February 2013 I set myself a project to photograph every rock pool in Sydney, resulting in this book and accompanying exhibition.

Sydney's coastline and harbour has a series of beautiful rock pools that have been cut into the base of cliffs and rocky headlands. Nearly every Sydney beach has one ocean pool which is usually located at the southern end, to give swimmers some protection when the southerly winds bring cold air and big seas. Some were built by wealthy people in the 1800s, others by convicts. They come in all shapes and sizes and each one has its own colourful history and interesting anecdotes.

In the five years I have spent in Sydney, I have seen many beautiful photographs of these rock pools from other photographers but I always wondered why no one had ever published a book about them. After a few months of intense shooting, I think I might have found the answer: it's hard work!

One of the challenges is being in the right place to shoot when the light, tide, swell and weather are just right. In photography, the best light occurs around dawn and sunset. High tides and big swell are also desirable conditions. Even with the best planning, sometimes it just doesn't work out!

My passion for both swimming and photography was the catalyst for this project. When I was young I was a swimmer in a small local swimming club in Spain and when I came to Sydney I had not swam seriously for 20 years. In October 2009, I settled at Dee Why beach and loved the sound and the smell of the ocean, the breaking waves and the Australian beach culture. I soon discovered that Australia is the most swimming-crazy country in the world and I became crazy about it too!

I am so glad this book has finally been published. Although it has been hard work, I have enjoyed every single moment. Being in solitude in the dark with my camera in front of the rock pools at sunrise is a magical experience. I am lucky to be able to say that I have seen sunrises and sunsets from every single beach in this beautiful city.

Mona Vale rock pool

Foreword

BY PETER EASTWAY

Some of my earliest memories are of swimming in Sydney's many rock pools, exploring the sandy bottoms, avoiding oysters under rusted metal ladders, floating on my back, eyes closed, enjoying the warmth of a summer sun.

Rock pools are not peculiar to Sydney, but they are an intrinsic part of our coastal heritage and a contemporary community hub. Frequent a pool for a few days and you'll observe a series of ordered patterns: the early risers doing laps, the dawdlers adjusting their bathing caps, the unattended dogs yapping at the water's edge. Rock pools accommodate many rituals, not just the ebb and flow of the tides.

Unlike our land-locked public baths with their rectangular grids and bright paint, these rock pools grow from their surroundings, melding and moulding with Sydney's sandstone coast. Straight lines and chain rails merge solidly into the natural erosion of our crumbling headlands, each pool unique, each full of character.

No doubt it is this character that has attracted photographer Ignacio Palacios to create his wonderful book of Sydney rock pool portraits. Stretching from Palm Beach in Sydney's north to Cronulla on the southern coast, Ignacio has explored each pool's individual character. Preferring the early mornings when the light is at its most tantalising, he has photographed our pools from every conceivable angle, including a series of dramatic aerials on a picture-postcard day.

While Sydney expands and grows, its progress marked by larger edifices and wider roads, Ignacio's photographs give us a sense of stability and timelessness. His images take us to quiet mornings spent distant from the hum and throb of traffic. Instead we hear the slap of an arm on smooth water, the wash of waves through a tangle of rocks, and early morning greetings as we share what is arguably Sydney's best secret.

Our rock pools.

Peter Eastway
Photographer, Collaroy

North Narrabeen rock pool

Northern Beaches

Palm Beach

Whale Beach

Avalon

Bungan

Bilgola

Newport

Mona Vale

Warriewood

Turrumetta

Narrabeen

Collaroy

Long Reef

Dee Why

Curl Curl

Freshwater

Manly

Eastern Suburbs

Bondi

Tamarama
Bronte

Clovelly

Coogee

Maroubra

Malabar

Long Bay

Little Bay

Palm Beach, the jewel of the Northern Beaches, is the northern most suburb of Sydney and its rock pool was built in the 1920s. It is 50 metres long and located at the southern end of Palm Beach in the area known as Kiddies Corner.

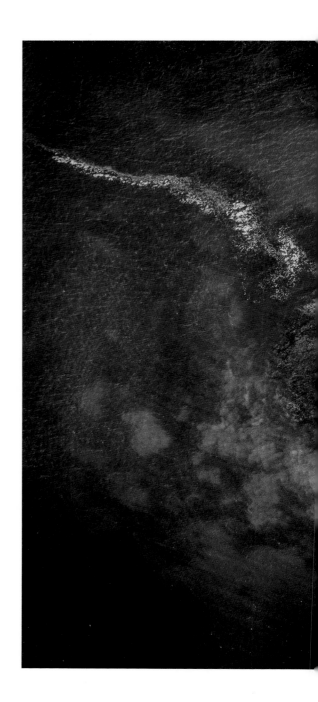

Whale Beach rock pool is situated at the southern end of the beach and can be accessed via The Strand. In the 1960s the Council deepened the pool in the hope it would self-fill. A pump was fitted, but then removed as it could not control the variable water supply. The rock pool is irregular in shape and has stone walls which give it a distinctive greenish colour.

Avalon Beach rock pool is located at the southern end of Avalon Beach. In the late 1920s rocks were blown up to expand the swimming area and walls were built. At that time, there was no pathway to the pool and the Norfolk Island pines were still saplings protected by tree guards.

In the 1920s there was a huge growth of amateur swimming clubs, an interest in aquatic sports, a move to mixed bathing on beaches and the use of ocean pools as training grounds for lifesavers.

In April 2011 a 1.5 metre baby bronze whaler shark was discovered cruising around inside the pool. Workers from Pittwater Council had to drain the pool before releasing it into the ocean.

Bilgola rock pool is located at the southern end of Bilgola Beach and it was built in the 1960s. The main pool is 50 metres by 15 metres and the wading pool is 50 metres by 5 metres. They are subdivided by a post-and-chain fence.

Erosion on the cliff made bathing a bit risky until Pittwater Council built high fences around the headland, so that rocks were less likely to fall on unsuspecting swimmers.

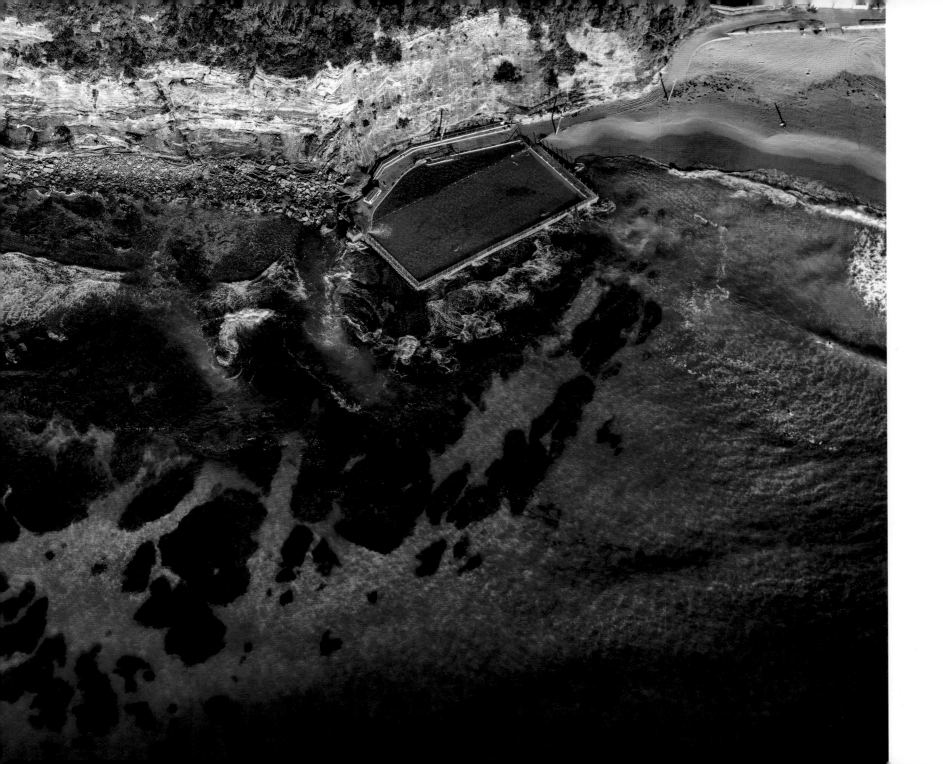

Newport rock pool is located on the rock platform at the southern end of Newport Beach. In the early 1900s Warringah Council constructed three rock pools at Newport. Two of them were situated at the northern end and one at the southern end of the beach. All were built with concrete and small rocks from the surrounds. Unfortunately they were too exposed to the elements and soon deteriorated.

After these first three ocean pools at Newport washed away, residents wanted another rock pool to be built. A new pool was constructed but during the following decades, there were numerous complaints to the Council about rock slides blocking the entrance. During World War II Newport was favoured by servicemen because it was the first beach north of Manly with no barbed-wire entanglements.

In 1966 the Newport Amateur Swimming Club succeeded in convincing the Council to enlarge the pool and to install a light for night swimming on the cliff top that overlooks the pool.

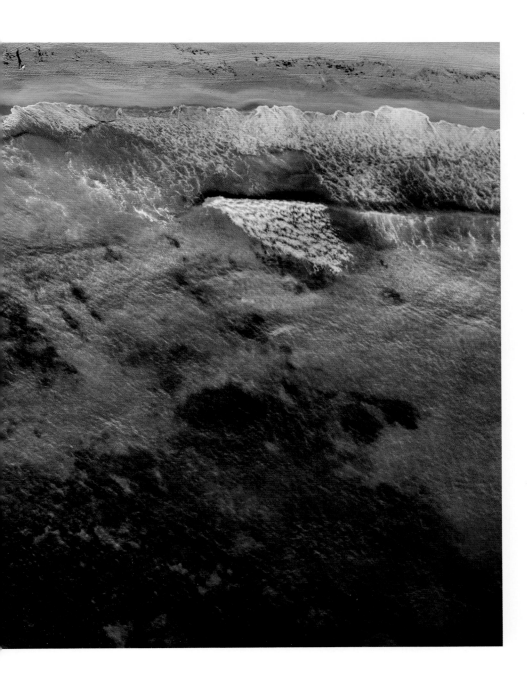

The pool was also frequented by wildlife. In 1985 around 30 dolphins spent two days surfing and feeding next to the pool and In August 2012 a humpback whale was washed up dead overnight. The 10 metre long, 20 tonnes 'juvenile' whale crushed the chains around it. When I saw this rock pool for the first time I did not think it was very photogenic, but together with Mona Vale and North Curl Curl it is now one of my favourite rock pools to photograph on the Northern Beaches. Interestingly, Max Dupain, a renowned Australian modernist photographer, created famous photographs of this pool in the 1930s and 1950s.

Mona Vale rock pool from the headland at sunset.

The 25 metre Mona Vale rock pool, built in the 1930s, is located on the tip of a sand spit on the rock shelf between Bongin Bongin Bay and Mona Vale Beach. When the tide is high, the pool is surrounded by the ocean making it look like an island. When the tide is lower and there aren't waves crashing over the pool, often the surface of the pool takes on a glassy tranquil look.

This is probably my favourite rock pool to photograph on the Northern Beaches. It is beautiful from either the land, sea or sky. I have been to this pool at sunrise and sunset more often than any other rock pool in Sydney.

The natural rock pool was enlarged as part of the Unemployment Relief Scheme. The pool was cut deep into the rock shelf to allow it to fill and empty while protecting it from the full force of the waves.

North Narrabeen rock pool is located at the entrance to Narrabeen Lagoon. The characteristic boardwalk between the pools is an original element and has been replaced many times.

The decking surrounds a 50 metre by 18-metre pool within a larger 70 metre by 40 metre pool, while the 60 metre by 50 metre pool reservoir acts as a wading pool.

The rock baths were constructed in the early 1930s under the Unemployment Relief Scheme and they were one of the largest and most unique rock pools in Sydney.

This photograph was taken at sunrise. A little bit of climbing and a few scratches were necessary to get the shot.

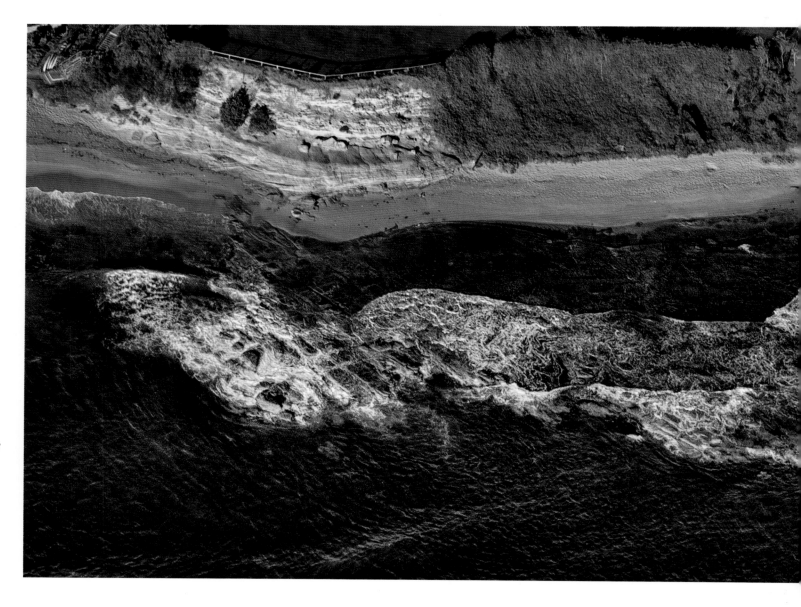

Collaroy rock pool is situated at the southern end of
Collaroy Beach. It is a classic ocean pool with chains
and two connecting pools. Both are irregular in shape
to follow the curvature of the nearby low-level rock
face promenade.

The ocean pool was officially opened in 1926 and
in 1937 work to deepen the rock pool and extend
its length to 50 metres was finalised under the
Unemployment Relief Scheme. In 1966 the rock pool
wall was rebuilt and step-ladders were constructed
on its northern and western walls.

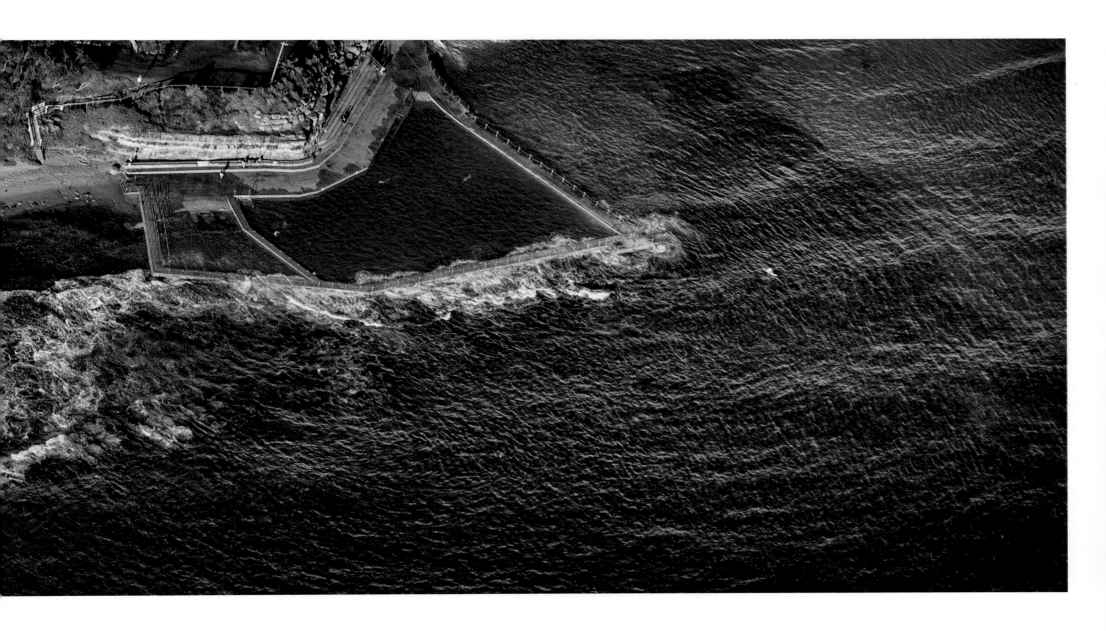

In the 1970s the Collaroy ocean pool was extended, its natural rock bottom concreted, exterior decking laid and public toilets built. The main pool was 50 metres by 25 metres, however, with no parallel walls, it remained impractical for swimming competitions and carnivals.

Dee Why pool is located at the southern end of Dee Why Beach and is easily accessed by the promenade walk. The complex contains two pools, the older main pool (50 metre) and a newer wading pool, formed by mass concrete walls integrating an outcrop of sandstone on one side.

In 1927 the baths were in the process of being expanded and the Dee Why Ladies Amateur Swimming Club donated 2 pounds to Warringah Council toward the cost of erecting a turning board in the pool, so swimmers did not have to turn on a rock face anymore. In the 1930s the main pool was 50 feet by 25 feet. When a working bee from the Dee Why men's club cleaned the pool, the Dee Why ladies club provided morning tea.

Between 1912 and 1915, members of the Dee Why Surf Club carved a pool by hand out of the rock shelf at the southern end of Dee Why Beach. On 14 February 1915, a Swimming Bath committee was formed and decided to ask Warringah Council to provide the funds to extend the original rock pool. On 27 December 1919 the enlarged baths were officially opened.

In the early 1940s, concerns of a Japanese invasion meant that Dee Why Beach, the reserve and the ladies clubhouse were surrounded by barbed-wire and anti-tank traps were placed on the beach. To obstruct the movement of enemy tanks, 30 timber piles were driven into sand.

In 1950 the Ladies Amateur Swimming Club had over 250 members and was the largest women's swimming club in Sydney. Nowadays, the Dee Why Ladies Amateur Swimming Club has become one of the oldest affiliated women's swimming clubs in Australia.

The establishment of daylight saving in 1972 meant Wednesday night club races were swum without artificial lighting.

North Curl Curl rock pool is a 32 metre by 20 metre rectangular, tidally flushed pool with two rock outcrops shaping an island within the pool. The natural rock shelf forms one side of the pool and it is reached by walking along the beach at low tide or climbing down a steep staircase from the headland.

In the early 1900s a natural rock pool was present in the rock platform below the Dee Why Head section where people used to camp. In the 1930s, under the Unemployment Relief Scheme, the North Curl Curl rock pool was built by extending the natural pool at a cost of 400 pounds. In 1947 the pool was severely damaged in a storm and it was not reconstructed until 1957.

South Curl Curl rock pool is a 50 metre tidally flushed pool at South Curl Curl Beach that was completed in 1926. During the 1930s, swimming in the rock pool was a popular activity for the children staying at Stewart House, a facility initiated to provide beach holiday housing for NSW schoolchildren 'from western suburbs and beyond'. In the late 1930s a wall was built in the rock pool, creating two pools. The external wall of the original rock pool is the centre wall of the current pool. The pool is also home to the Frigid Frogs Club which runs all year round.

In 1966 the rock pool was shortened to provide Olympic standards for 50 metre competitions. This created a pool compound that consisted of a 'stilling basin', a main pool (50 metres by 12 metres) and a wading pool of 25 metres by 15 metres. In 1990 a deck was attached onto the clubhouse to extend the room available for the Frigid Frogs Club. In 1997 the children's pool was partly concreted, entry ramps were established and pool walls restored.

There is a group of retired locals who is often seen sunning themselves by the pool, affectionately known as 'the walruses'.

Freshwater rock pool is located at the northern end of Harbord's Freshwater Beach and was the first rock pool to be constructed on the Northern Beaches (1925) at a total cost of 472 pounds. It was built on an excavated rock platform with tiered seating along the full length of the pool. When the pool was opened on 28 November 1925, it measured 33 yards (30.18 metres).

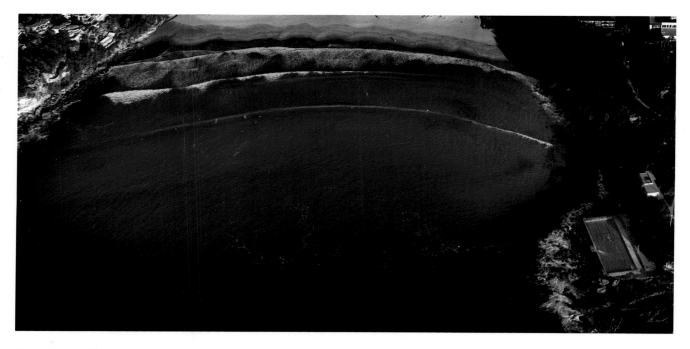

The pool was used for swimming competitions by lifesavers and in 1962, to meet with the standard for competition swimming pools, it was extended from 33 to 55 yards (50 metres) at the western end. Funnily, in 1999 a baptism took place at the pool in front of hundreds of people.

Queenscliff rock pool is located at the northern end of Queenscliff Beach, a short walk north of Manly Beach. This pool is shallow and has sides that are not parallel, but is still a considerable swimming pool (50 metre by 14 metre) with clear marked lanes and a swimming club . The pool is cut into the rock platform and has formed concrete walls on all sides.

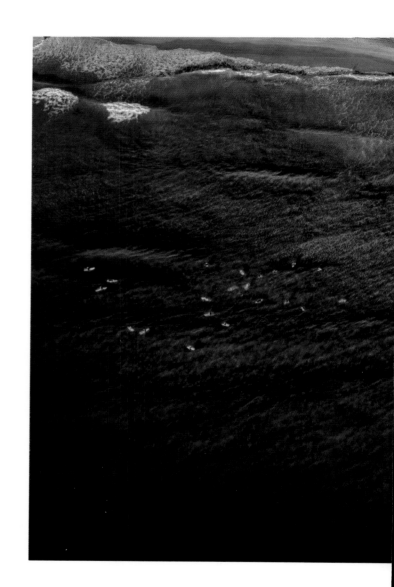

In 1937 the rock pool was built by unemployed labour as part of the Unemployment Relief Scheme. Manly Council was constructing a stone wall along the ocean front (North Steyne) and was prepared to take any stone from the excavation for the Queenscliff rock pool. The QSLSC (Queenscliff Surf Life Saving Club) maintained the pool for a few years, before Council took over this responsibility. In 1985 the Queenscliff pool was included as a heritage item on the draft Warringah Local Environmental Plan after the Warringah Heritage Inventory review identified it as having State or regional significance with the themes of 'leisure: organised and unorganised' and 'cultural and social life'.

Fairy Bower rock pool is the first ocean baths to the north of Sydney Harbour and is located in Manly's Cabbage Tree Bay. The Fairy Bower pool is tiny and triangular in shape, one of the smallest and newest public rock pools in Sydney.

In 1997 a sculpture known as The Oceanids was established at the side of the pool. The pool is an attractive spot for people walking between Manly and Shelly beach.

In the 1920s professional and recreational fisherman kept their boats on Shelly Beach next to Fairy Bower Beach. Fish guts in the water brought sharks prompting locals to build a shark-netted enclosure and encourage the erection of a rock pool.

This tidal rock pool was the first of its kind south of Sydney Harbour. It is located next to a popular rock fishing spot. The original pool was a swimming spot created by residents. Later it was formally named after Wally Weekes, a publican, boxer and patron of the North Bondi Surf Club.

This wading pool is located below the Biddigal Reserve at North Bondi, next to Wally Weekes Pool. Until 1947 it was known as the Mermaid Pool. There is a mosaic wall running along one side of the pool featuring beautiful sea images. This was largely made by volunteers as a community arts project.

Sydney's most famous beach is Bondi and Bondi Icebergs Pool is arguably the most famous ocean pool in Australia.

With a length of 50 metres and eight lanes, this is a great pool to train in. It opens every day except Thursdays and it is home to Australia's best-known winter swimming club – the Bondi Icebergs Club, which was founded in 1929 by a small group of friends.

Icebergs members earn their place by swimming three out of every four Sundays during winter for five years. In winter the ocean water is already teeth-chattering cold but on the opening day of winter it is tradition to throw ice into the pool to further test the endurance and hardiness of the swimmers. Women have only been allowed to join Icebergs since 1994 and there are now 350 members.

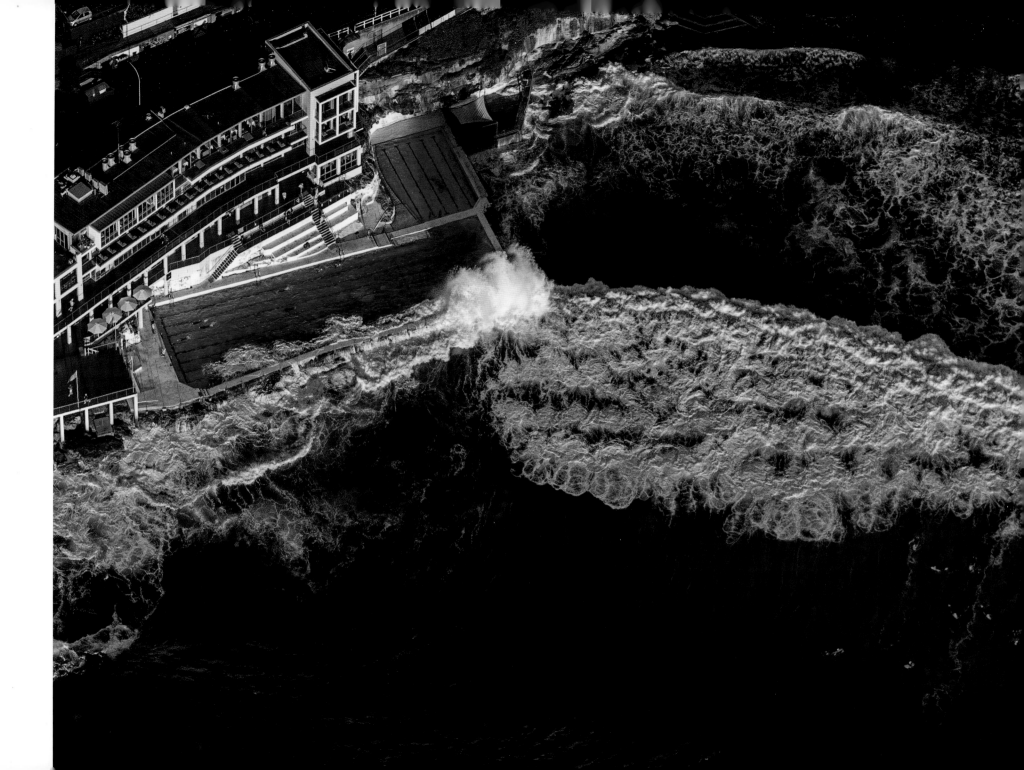

Bronte Bogey Hole is located at the southern end of Bronte Beach close to the more popular Bronte Baths. The rock pool is a modified 'natural' Bogey Hole, a ring of rocks with a hole at its centre. In the early 1880s the Bogey Hole was a popular bathing place before Waverley Council gained permission to construct the Bronte Baths nearby.

In 1996 a pod of about 15 dolphins jumped into the Bogey Hole and frolicked about to the delight of onlookers. In 2001 a man was swimming in the Bronte Bogey Hole when he was bitten by a gummy shark. He went to hospital with the shark still attached to his arm. Later he took the shark home for dinner.

Bronte Baths are located at the southern end of Bronte Beach. The baths are also known as the Bond Ocean Pool after swimming teacher, Major Bond. The pool is very photogenic and has been the subject of many photographers and artists. It has featured on postcards since the early 1900s.

 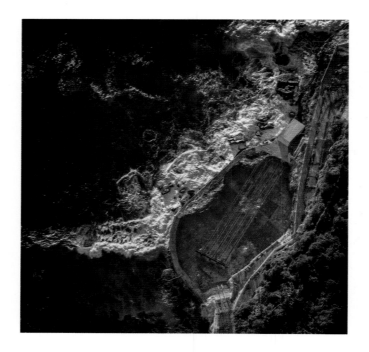

In 1887 the Bronte Baths was opened for segregated bathing. The regulations stated that gentlemen could bathe between daylight and 10 am and from 4 pm till dark each day. Ladies were welcome from 10 am to 4 pm daily except on Sundays and Public Holidays, when the baths were reserved exclusively for men from daylight to dark. Each person using the baths should wear an appropriate bathing dress. Baths' entry cost four pence for an adult.

In 1921 the Bronte Splashers Swimming Club was created. Its goals included creating 'a friendly feeling of goodwill between all beach and baths swimmers', holding swimming competitions and arranging get-togethers and functions for its members. Winter swimming was a popular activity of the club and around 1939 the pool was modified for lap and competition swimming by using a turning board to define a rectangular course within the pool.

A pool within a pool, the Clovelly ocean baths form part of Sydney's only concreted swimming beach and is located in the promenade on the southern shore of Clovelly Bay. This rectangular 25 metre pool with marked lanes lies next to the generally peaceful waters of the bay.

In the 1930s the Council published plans to build an Olympic sized swimming pool and a sea wall using unemployed labour. Various attempts were made to build a breakwater across the mouth of the bay but the plans were modified after winter storms destroyed most of the sea wall, leaving only a protective rocky reef now visible at low tide.

In 1953 the Clovelly Winter Swimming Club was founded by Clovelly surf club members and used Clovelly Bay as their swimming pool. In 1962, Geoff James of the Clovelly surf club proposed the building of a concrete swimming pool and in 2002 Randwick Council named the pool after him. The Clovelly Eskimos winter swimming club has about 125 members, most of whom are in their forties or older.

A gate on the cliff with the words 'Baths' on the north side of Coogee Bay leads to steps down to a small natural rock pool which has long been a popular swimming place. The pool was originally known as the Bogey Hole, but was later renamed Dolphin Point in memory of the six members of the Coogee Dolphins A Grade Rugby League team, who were killed on October 12 2002 when two bombs exploded in a nightclub in Bali. Now there is a plaque listing the names of twenty locals who died in the bombing.

In the early 1900s these baths were known as Lloyds Baths. Lloyds Baths banned dogs and swearing and required bathers to wear swimming trunks. The Baths were advertised as 'one of the few baths where the healthful past time of sun baking may be indulged in'.

In 1929 the baths changed names when Oscar E. Giles opened the 'Giles Hot Sea Baths and Swimming Pool' on the site of the former Lloyds Baths as part of the November 'Come to Coogee' week celebrations. Giles was a massage therapist and the Giles Baths offered a range of therapies to men and women in separate facilities. But only men could swim in the rock pool naked. The Giles Baths served as a 'genteel beat' for Sydney's gay men. In the 1960s the baths' entry fee of 20 cents provided access to a locker and the chance to sunbake nude in the enclosed yard at the back of the bathhouse.

In 1975 the baths were renovated and re-opened as Giles Health Centre. Women could now use the rock pool and all of the amenities other than the hot sea baths which were frequented by jockeys from Randwick racecourse needing to lose weight. Pool patrons (90% men) included a broad spectrum of society including sportsmen, police, members of the judiciary, criminals and gay men.

In 2000 the baths were demolished but the portico which once formed the entrance to the Giles Baths was conserved.

In 2003 apparitions of the Virgin Mary were reported near Giles Baths, and it became a place of pilgrimage, drawing lots of people.

Coogee Ross Jones Memorial Pool has walls similar to the top of a sand castle and is situated next to the Coogee Surf Club. The Coogee Penguins and the Coogee Huskies, two winter swimming clubs are connected with this pool.

The pool was built in 1947 by Randwick Council and funded by a compensation payment from the Commonwealth government to Council for war-time damage to Randwick's beaches. This was a total amount of 963 pounds plus a further 350 pounds for the protective walls.

The Coogee Penguins Club, which swam there on winter Sunday mornings, promoted itself as a family club with an equal numbers of male and female members.

McIver's Baths at Coogee Beach is the last-remaining 'women and children only' seawater pool in Australia. It was built in 1886 and has been in continuous use since its establishment.

This gorgeous 20 metre ocean pool is set on the rock platform between the Coogee Surf Club and Wylies Baths. Overlooking the sea, the baths are a private space surrounded by native coastal vegetation and small grassed areas, well screened from passers-by walking along the Grant Reserve above the pool.

Built in the 1800s, it was long known as the 'nun's pool'. Today, Muslim women are more often seen, together with pregnant women and older women. In the early nineteenth century the pool site may have been a traditional bathing place for Aboriginal women.

The McIver family ran the baths until 1922 when the Randwick Ladies Amateur Swimming Club was formed. Free swimming lessons have been provided at the pool since that time. Until 1994 only boys under 7 were permitted at the swimming lessons but they are now allowed up to age 12.

In 1946 Randwick Council decided to apply to the Minister for Lands to have the baths available to the public for mixed bathing. The decision was overturned after objections from the Mother Superior of the Brigidine Convent at Randwick, stating that the nuns at her convent as well as any country nuns vacationing there would not be able to visit the baths if they were opened for mixed bathing. In 1972 Council discussed plans to build a solid fence around the pool to deter 'perverts and peek-a-boos'. In 2014 the pool entry fee was 20 cents. Club members pay 50 cents as a fundraising measure.

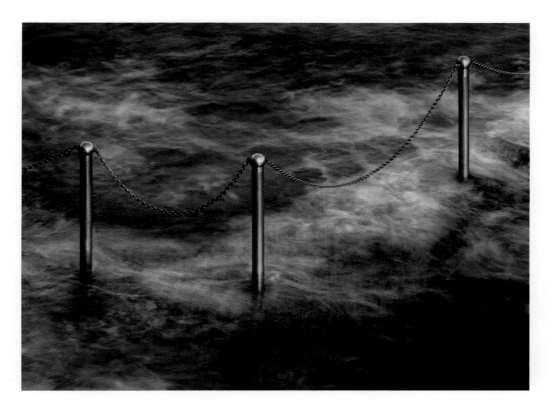

Wylie's Baths in Coogee is one of the most popular ocean pools in the area. It is south of McIver's Baths and is open 365 days a year, but the opening hours vary by season. A fee of $4.80 is charged for adults and $2.20 for children and students. Henry Alexander Wylie, a champion long distance swimmer, established Wylies Baths in 1907. The pool is 35 metres by 45 metres and was named after Mina Wylie (Henry's daughter) who won a silver medal in swimming at the 1912 Olympic games. It is located a few hundred metres south of Coogee Beach below the coast track between Coogee and Maroubra. The baths have 180 degree views of the Pacific Ocean overlooking the famous Wedding Cake Island. The baths were one of the first mixed gender bathing pools in Australia.

Sometimes, when there is big swell, the waves crash over the edge of the pool making it impossible to maintain lane etiquette as swimmers crash into each other. As with most rock pools, it has its own club of locals, men and women of all ages who swim there regularly and compete on Sundays.

This is a tiny pool accessed by steep steps from the coastal walkway. In the 1940s this rock pool was popular with local children and in 1965 the site's main natural pool was enlarged. From 1965 to the early 1980s local residents kept the pool clean and the seaweed they took out made this spot well known by local fishermen for catching blackfish.

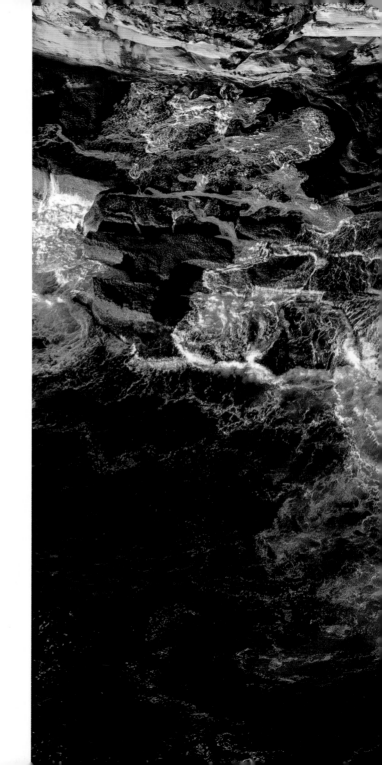

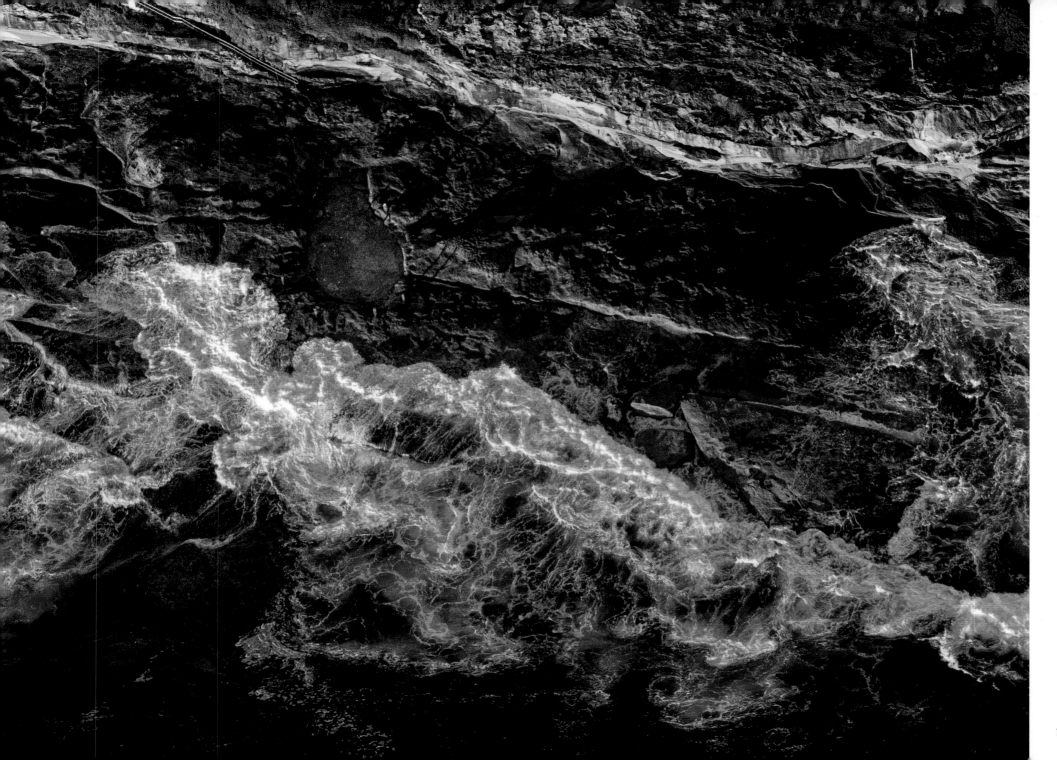

Mahon rock pool is located north of Maroubra Beach and it was built in 1932 by Randwick Council as an Unemployment Relief project. It is cut into the rock and has a wonderfully natural feel to it which makes it very popular among photographers.

In 1988 the Mahon pool was in terrible condition and two separate petitions with a combined total of 313 signatures were presented to Randwick Council by locals urging improvements which were delayed by a year because of rough seas. Extensive repairs were carried out and in 1994 the National Trust classified the Mahon pool and listed it on its heritage register.

In the late 1920s Maroubra Surf Club constructed these rock pools at the southern end of Maroubra Beach. The rock pools have had some issues with water quality but the they are now safe for swimming. A bit complicated to photograph from land, the most beautiful way to capture these pools is from the air.

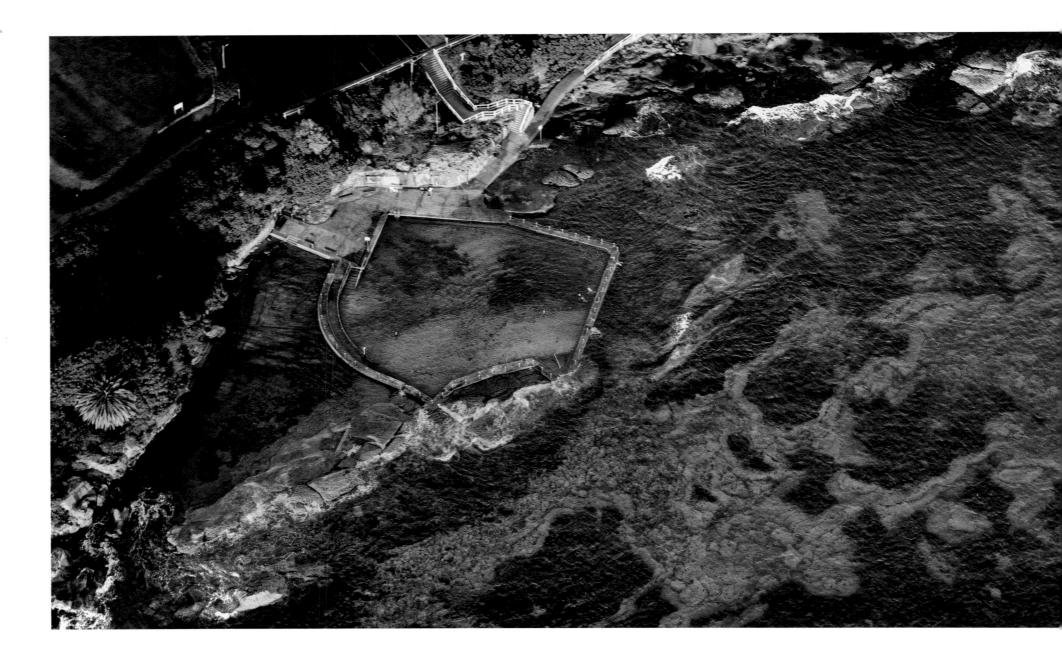

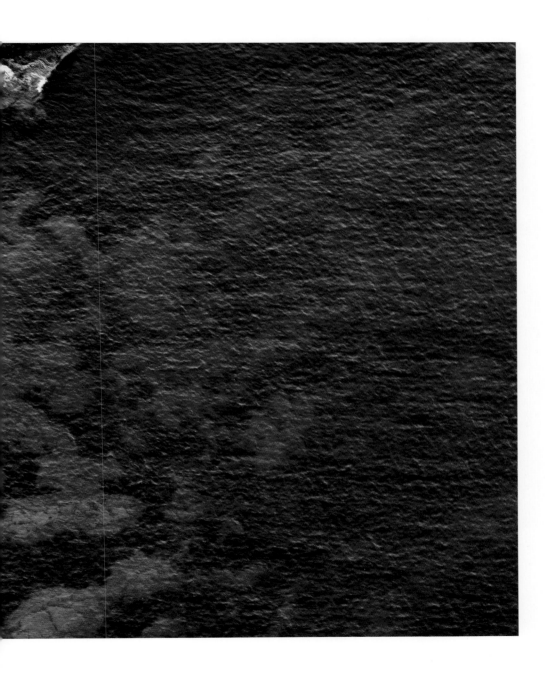

Malabar rock pool is in Long Bay, below the Randwick Golf Club. In the 1890s a rock pool formed with boulders existed on the southside of Long Bay, but it had issues with sewage pollution. In 1997 it was restored, reopened and now the water quality is excellent.

This pool was built with beach rocks and is located on the south tip of Little Bay in the grounds of the Prince Henry Hospital. In the early 1900s the hospital's nurses enjoyed swimming at the beach in Little Bay, often at night. After several shark sightings, Matron Jean McMaster forbade the nurses to swim there but that didn't stop them. There were no shark fatalities but in 1905 the rock pool in Little Bay was constructed as a 'safe' swimming spot for nurses.

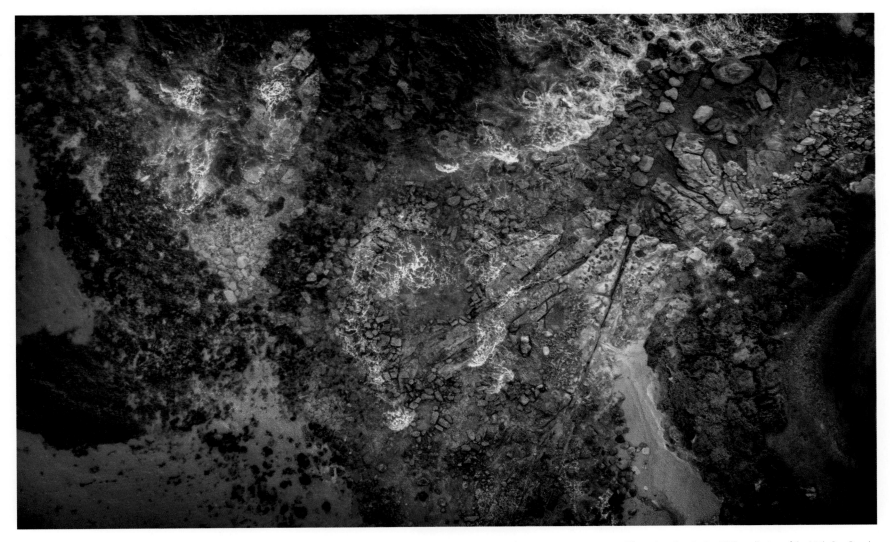

Nurses at the hospital still paddled at the Little Bay Beach but in the 1970s waste from sewage outfall to the north made the water too contaminated for swimming. In the 1990s pollution of the Little Bay Beach and rock pool was prevented by construction of a deep-ocean outfall at Malabar.

DIVING
PROHIBITED

Acknowledgements

I would like to thank and acknowledge the following organisations and people for their contribution to this book and for making me a better photographer and swimmer!

• Phil Hatten, Mark Hunt, David Murray from the FF squad in St. Leonards, Jeff and Louise Price and Mark Patterson from the Seaside Pirates Master Club and Hamid Mobarred at the Ian Thorpe Aquatic Centre. They all helped me break the minute in the 100 freestyle and go to the Masters World Championships in Italy in 2012. I have greatly enjoyed your friendship and competing with you in the pool and the ocean for the last 5 years;

• Lucy Murray, my wife, who supported me during the whole process; taking care of our kids while I was out shooting in the mornings and evenings and for helping edit this book;

• The Sydney Morning Herald, the Gaffa Gallery, Better Photography Magazine, Epson Australia and all Councils: Pittwater Council, Warringah Council, Manly Council, Waverley Council, Randwick Council and Sutherland Shire Council, for their support of this project and

• The NSW Heritage Office and NSW Ocean Baths websites.

I would also like to thank:

Peter Eastway for helping out with some images that were proving difficult to process with Photoshop and for joining me in a helicopter to shoot the amazing Sydney coastline on a truly beautiful morning. Thanks also for writing the foreword of my book. In the last 5 years I have grown as a photographer with your advice and guidance. Thanks also to Kathie Eastway for your beautiful design.

Most photographs in this book were captured with a Pentax 645D medium format digital camera, high-end lenses and professional equipment. With 40 effective megapixels, this camera produces extra-sharp, super-high-resolution images.

For this book I have used the 55 mm f2.8 AL (IF) SDM AW and 25 mm F4AL [IF] SDM AW lenses.

In addition I have also used the Pentax SMCP-FA FA 645 300 mm F/4.0 and the Pentax FA 645 120mm f/4 MACRO. These two lenses were a great addition to photograph some of the pools from the headlands and to capture some smaller details.

All images were worked in Photoshop CS6. Other post processing software used included PTGui, Helicon Focus, NIK Software and Adobe Camera Raw. For this purpose, I used a calibrated Eizo monitor CG241W.

Most photographs in the book were taken either at sunset or sunrise and using a tripod Gitzo GT1541T with a Markins head Q3 Emille Travel and a Really Right Stuff Sliding Panoramic package MPR-CL II Nodal Slide and PCL-1 Panning Clamp.

Some of the photographs in this book were exhibited in Sydney as limited edition prints.

If you are interested in purchasing a print, please go to my website at *www.iptravelphotography.com.au*.